100% UNOFFICIAL

# MR BEAST

## THE ULTIMATE FAN BOOK

Published in the UK by Scholastic, 2024
1 London Bridge, London, SE1 9BG
Scholastic Ireland, 89E Lagan Road, Dublin Industrial Estate, Glasnevin, Dublin, D11 HP5F
SCHOLASTIC and associated logos are trademarks and/or registered trademarks of Scholastic Inc.

Text by Claire Sipi © Scholastic, 2024
Designed by Cloud King Creative
Photography © Getty Images

ISBN 978 0702 33475 7

A CIP catalogue record for this book is available from the British Library.

All rights reserved.
This book is sold subject to the condition that it shall not, by way of trade or otherwise, be lent, hired out or otherwise circulated in any form of binding or cover other than that in which it is published. No part of this publication may be reproduced, stored in a retrieval system, or transmitted in any form or by any other means (electronic, mechanical, photocopying, recording or otherwise) without prior written permission of Scholastic Limited.

The publisher does not have any control over and does not assume any responsibility for the views, thoughts, and opinions of those individuals featured in this book.

Printed and bound in China by C&C Offset Printing Co., Ltd.

Paper made from wood grown in sustainable forests and other controlled sources.

1 3 5 7 9 10 8 6 4 2

www.scholastic.co.uk

100% UNOFFICIAL

# MR BEAST

## THE ULTIMATE FAN BOOK

WRITTEN BY CLAIRE SIPI

**SCHOLASTIC**

# CONTENTS

- LET'S GO ............................................. 7
- THE MRBEAST FILES ........................ 8
- YOUTUBE: THE EARLY YEARS ......... 10
- YOUTUBE: GOING VIRAL .................. 14
- YOUTUBE: MEGASTAR! ..................... 18
- THE MRBEAST CHANNELS ............... 22
- MRBEAST AND MRBEAST 2 ............. 24
- CHALLENGES, STUNTS AND BIG-MONEY GIVEAWAYS ................ 26
- THE BEAST GANG .............................. 38
- BEAST REACTS ................................... 42
- BEAST GAMING .................................. 43
- BEAST PHILANTHROPY ..................... 44
- #TEAMTREES ...................................... 46
- #TEAMSEAS ........................................ 48
- BEAST BUSINESS ............................... 50
- FEASTABLES ....................................... 54
- AND THE WINNER IS . . . ? ............... 56
- THE MAN BEHIND THE BEAST ........ 58
- PICTURE CREDITS .............................. 64

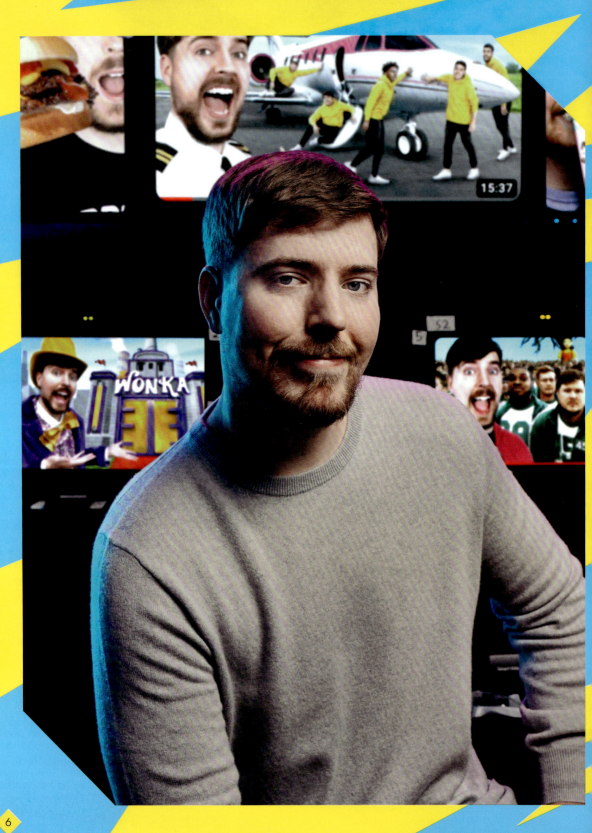

# LET'S GO

If you've ever wondered how the much-loved megastar MrBeast became one of the **BIGGEST** and **most popular** YouTubers on the planet, then you've picked up the right book! Read on to discover everything there is to know about the digital hero.

From a little-known, shy 13-year-old YouTuber to one of the most influential video creators of his time, Jimmy Donaldson, better known as **MrBeast**, is an internet phenomenon with his own unique style and brand.

Follow his incredible journey and learn how he turned his love of online gaming and his fascination with the digital world (and especially YouTube!) into a multi-million dollar brand.

## KING OF THE PLATFORM!

MrBeast is all over the internet, especially on YouTube, the channel that shot him to fame! His fans keep up with his latest stunts, challenges and philanthropy via his social-media handles **MrBeast** or **@MrBeast**.

## STAY SAFE ONLINE

YouTube, X (formerly known as Twitter), Instagram, Snapchat, TikTok and other social media platforms have a minimum age requirement to use them. They can be loads of fun and a great way to keep up with your favourite celebs, or stay in touch with friends and family. However, it's important to be smart and stay safe online.

**NEVER** give out personal details such as your full name, address, phone number or school. Don't ask anyone for these details, either.

**DON'T** post photos that might give away the location of your home or school.

**REPORT** any comments that make you feel uncomfortable to a trusted adult.

**DON'T** ignore the age restrictions on social media platforms – these are there for your own safety.

**RESPECT** other users, including those who have different views and opinions to you.

# THE MRBEAST FILES

**NAME:** James Stephen Donaldson ("Jimmy" for short)

**YOUTUBE NAME:** MrBeast

**DATE OF BIRTH:** 7 May, 1998

**ZODIAC SIGN:** Taurus

**BORN IN:** Wichita, Kansas, USA

**GREW UP IN:** Greenville, North Carolina, USA

**BROTHER:** Charles "C.J." Donaldson (two years older and also a YouTuber)

**FAMOUS FOR:** being a YouTuber, entrepreneur and philanthropist*, and credited with pioneering a genre of YouTube videos that centre on expensive challenges and stunts, plus generous giveaways

**SOCIAL MEDIA AND WEBSITES:** YouTube (MrBeast, MrBeast 2, MrBeast Gaming, Beast Reacts, Beast Philanthropy); Instagram, X (formerly Twitter) and TikTok @MrBeast; mrbeaststore.com (for merch); feastables.com; mrbeastburger.com

**YEARS ACTIVE:** 2012 to present (and still going strong!)

*a person who seeks to promote the welfare of others, especially by the generous donation of money to good causes.

"I'm living the life I would dream of every night when I was 13. I love you all and thank you so much for watching our videos!!! I'll never take you all for granted."

## DID YOU KNOW?

MrBeast ended the reign of Pewdiepie (AKA Felix Kjellberg) as the most-subscribed YouTube creator ever on 14 November, 2022, when he overtook Pewdiepie's 111,846,079 subscribers.

# YouTube
## THE EARLY YEARS

Like a lot of young teenagers, Jimmy was an avid gamer and spent many hours watching YouTube videos. He was fascinated by how a social media platform could connect people from all over the world, and how they could share their ideas and stories.

As a self-confessed introvert, Jimmy saw potential for someone like himself to use the platform to **express their personality** and **showcase their creativity**.

### DID YOU KNOW?

Although Jimmy dropped out of college, as MrBeast he once taught a class at the famous Harvard Business School.

> **"Just do what makes you happy and people will find your brand eventually."**

So, in 2012, a few months after his 14th birthday, Jimmy set up a YouTube account under the handle **MrBeast6000** and started posting content. He began with gaming content where he played and commented on some of the more popular online games of the time, such as **Minecraft** and **Call of Duty: Black Ops II**. Jimmy rarely appeared on screen himself in his early videos.

Although he didn't have hundreds of views or subscribers, Jimmy's early videos allowed him to understand what his audience wanted, to experiment with his presentations and to learn how YouTube worked. He spent many hours studying other successful YouTubers to see what they did and didn't do well.

A perfectly pixelated MrBeast skin from *Minecraft*.

> **" I would stay up all night just thinking of ideas. "**

Over the next few years, Jimmy experimented with different types of content, from his "Let's Play" gaming commentaries to videos estimating the wealth of other YouTubers and even ones that offered tips to upcoming YouTubers.

**EAT SLEEP GAME REPEAT**

### DID YOU KNOW?

MrBeast says he **does not remember much of his childhood**, explaining that it is because he likes to **focus on the future**. His mum, Sue, meanwhile, has a warehouse full of keepsakes from his early years and footage of his oldest YouTube videos.

During 2015 and 2016, Jimmy gained popularity with his "Worst intros on YouTube" series where he poked good-humoured fun at video intros posted by other creators. It was at this point – having grown his subscribers to around 30,000 – that 18-year-old Jimmy decided to become a full-time YouTuber with his MrBeast channel.

> **❞ I am motivated because I want to be a YouTuber. ❞**

# YouTube
## GOING VIRAL

As a full-time YouTuber, MrBeast put in long working hours creating a lot of content and trying out new things, such as attempting to break Guinness World Records. He included some stunts in his videos, like trying to break glass using the **NOISE from 100 megaphones** (DON'T try this at home!), while in another he **watched paint dry for an hour** (ZZZZZZZ . . .)!

> **"I want to make YouTube videos until the day I die, I love this so much."**

Then in 2017, Jimmy uploaded a video in which he **counted to 100,000**! The video took about 40 hours to make, but he reduced it to a 24-hour-long video by speeding up some sections of his counting. Within just a few days, this **video went viral**. Suddenly, MrBeast was catapulted into the social media spotlight. This was the beginning of his incredible rise to fame as one of the world's most successful YouTubers. The rest, as they say, is history!

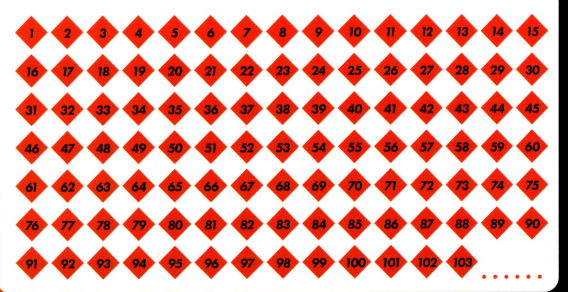

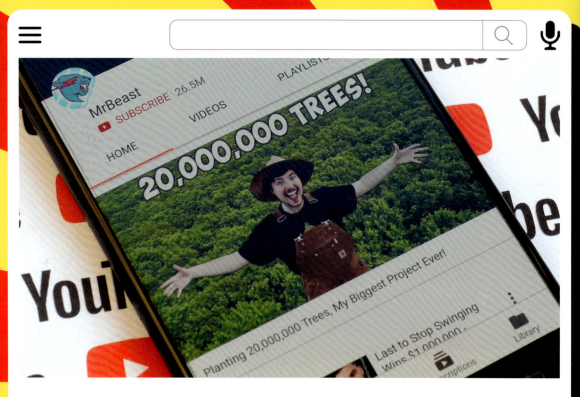

MrBeast's new viral status on YouTube brought in more sponsors to help fund his videos. This allowed him to produce better content; he was able to film more extravagant stunts, to invent innovative challenges and to give away **thousands of dollars** to individuals or good causes. Whether MrBeast is tipping hundreds of dollars to pizza-delivery drivers, paying people to take part in bizarre challenges, pranking his friends or contributing to environmental causes, he knows how to **engage his audience** and leave them wanting more.

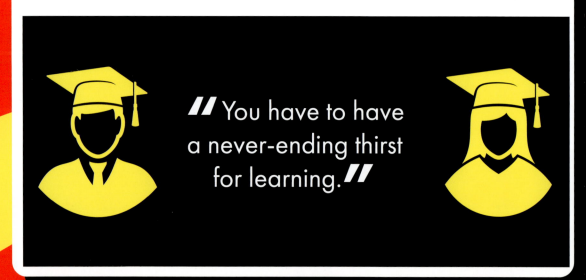

"You have to have a never-ending thirst for learning."

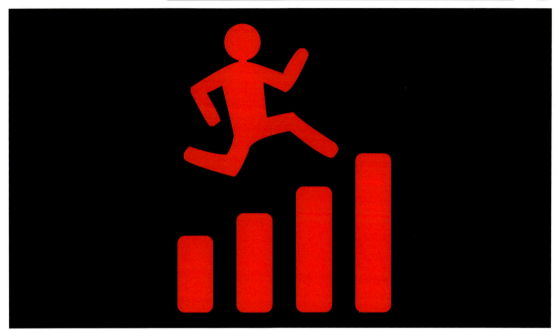

Such a meteoric rise to fame comes with many challenges and pressures, but Jimmy rose to the occasion. He worked harder and had more fun. He stayed true to his unique brand of entertainment. Jimmy continues to produce **must-watch content** to keep his viewers locked-in and his material relevant.

At the heart of all Jimmy's work is the desire to always be generous and **make a difference in people's lives**. His content must do more than entertain, it should make his audience feel good, and push the boundaries of what is considered possible on YouTube.

By 2018, MrBeast had given away over **$1,000,000** through his stunts and challenges, earning him the title of **"YouTube's biggest philanthropist"**.

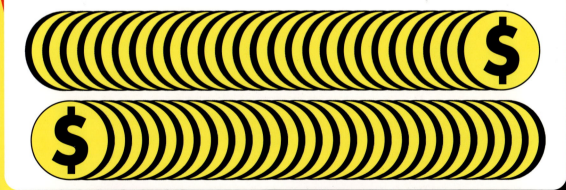

# YouTube MEGASTAR!

To stay at the top of his game, Jimmy knows that he must keep creating content that will go viral. Combining his **philanthropy** with his **high-stakes challenges** is key to his success.

People love a **heart-warming story** where someone is given a life-changing sum of money or rises to overcome a difficult challenge, just as much as they love watching a Lamborghini being shredded or a huge metal tube being dropped on expensive objects! It makes for content that is seriously shareable. Positivity, charitable endeavours and quirky, fun stunts = more clicks and likes online!

Since 2017, MrBeast has maintained his global viral status via his videos including:

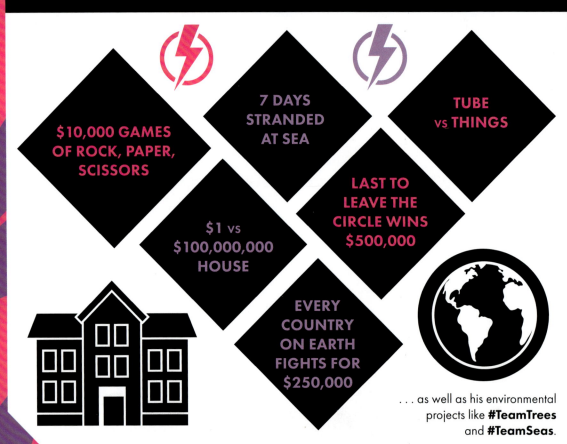

- $10,000 GAMES OF ROCK, PAPER, SCISSORS
- 7 DAYS STRANDED AT SEA
- TUBE vs THINGS
- $1 vs $100,000,000 HOUSE
- LAST TO LEAVE THE CIRCLE WINS $500,000
- EVERY COUNTRY ON EARTH FIGHTS FOR $250,000

. . . as well as his environmental projects like **#TeamTrees** and **#TeamSeas**.

# $456,000 REAL LIFE SQUID GAME
○ □ △

MrBeast's 2022 video "$456,000 Real Life Squid Game" (a recreation and parody of the popular Netflix *Squid Game* TV series), in which 456 people competed for a cash prize, is his most watched video, with more than 500 million views . . . and counting!

## CELEB ROCK, PAPER, SCISSORS!

MrBeast challenged Dwayne "The Rock" Johnson to the ultimate rock, paper, scissors competition, with the loser promising to pledge $100,000 to charity. MrBeast won!

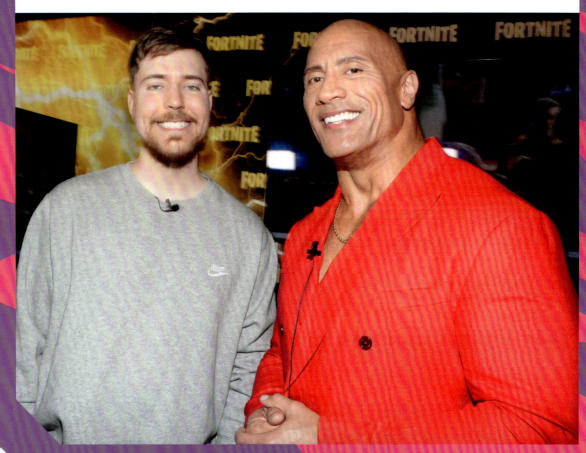

# MRBEAST STATS

More than **219 million** subscribers.

Top 3 videos that broke the record for the most YouTube views (for a non-music video) in a 24-hour period:
- 7 Days Stranded at Sea
- $1 vs $250,000 Vacation
- Every Country on Earth Fights for $250,000

Most-subscribed independent producer on YouTube.

*Time* magazine named MrBeast as one of the world's 100 most influential people in 2023.

Ranked **#1** on Forbes list for highest-earning YouTube creator in 2022, earning a whopping $54 million (£43 million). As of early 2024, he was the highest-paid YouTuber, worth an estimated $500 million (£396 million).

More than **38 billion** video views.

**Top 5 most-watched videos:**
**#5** $1 vs $1,000,000 Hotel Room
**#4** I Spent 50 Hours in Solitary Confinement
**#3** I Spent 50 Hours Buried Alive
**#2** Last to Leave the Circle Wins $500,000
**#1** $456,000 Squid Game in Real Life!

# THE MRBEAST CHANNELS

As you know, MrBeast is active across most social media platforms, including Instagram, TikTok, X (formerly Twitter) and Facebook. But his true home is YouTube, where he has five main channels:

| | | JOINED: |
|---|---|---|
| 2012 | MRBEAST | 20 February |
| 2016 | BEAST REACTS | 24 April |
| 2020 | BEAST GAMING | 7 April |
| 2020 | MRBEAST 2 | 21 August |
| 2020 | BEAST PHILANTHROPY | 18 September |

**MrBeast** and **MrBeast 2** are Jimmy's main channels for all his challenges, stunts, pranks, giveaway videos and shorts.

**Beast Reacts** has loads of epic videos of MrBeast and co-host Kris reacting to the internet's favourite videos, such as the rarest things on Earth, the funniest animals on the internet or the fastest onion ever eaten! OKKKK!

**MrBeast Gaming** focuses on video games, including super-tough challenges in **Minecraft** and **GTA**.

**Beast Philanthropy** is for all of MrBeast's charitable projects, and where 100% of the profits from the adverts, merch sales and sponsorships go towards making the world a better place. What's not to like?

> I think on YouTube, it's different, and people just haven't realized it: positivity is just as clickbait as negativity.

# MRBEAST AND MRBEAST 2

**SUBSCRIBE FOR A COOKIE!**

MrBeast's "$100,000 Finger on the App" game challenged players to keep their finger on a specially created app for as long as possible! Four contestants each won **$20,000!**

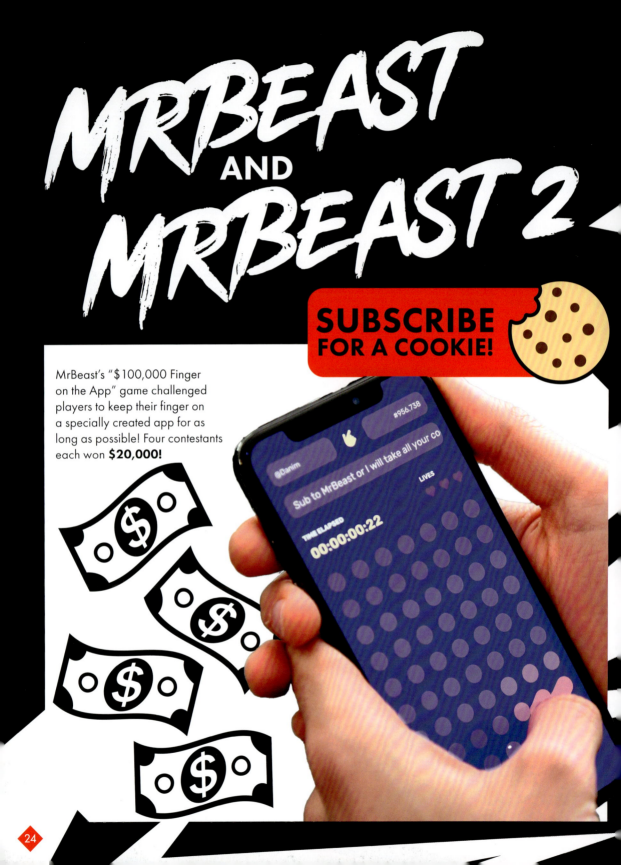

> **"You should make content that makes people feel good about themselves."**

**MrBeast** and **MrBeast 2** channels are the home of MrBeast's high-stakes challenges, stunts, pranks and big-dollar giveaways, videos and shorts. Whether MrBeast is comparing a $1 house to a $100,000,000 house, giving $500,000 to the last person to leave a circle, floating on a raft at sea with his friends for seven days or feeding a cat $10 vs $10,000 sushi, he knows how to keep his audience engaged and coming back for more.

The titles of his videos are designed to reel in viewers (and go viral) by promising outrageous stunts or competitions using key words like "challenge" or "24 hours", and by offering up large sums of money. Each video is typically 10–20 minutes long; time enough to include all the gang's wacky challenges or stunts on elaborate sets, but not too long to lose his fans' attention. The shorts are, well . . . as the name suggests, short – under a minute long, where Jimmy does something quite ordinary like making an egg sandwich with @BayashiTV but in a highly entertaining and funny way!

Most of MrBeast's funding for his extravagant videos, with sets and locations costing thousands of dollars, comes from sponsors and advertisers on the YouTube channel. MrBeast also uses his **Beast Reacts** and **Beast Gaming** channels to help fund his main channel. Money that MrBeast earns from his businesses: MrBeast merch, MrBeast Burger and Feastables, helps him maintain the high-quality production of all his content.

> **"One of the reasons I like giving away money is I just like to see how people react."**

# CHALLENGES, STUNTS AND BIG-MONEY GIVEAWAYS

Whether it's the deadliest, most dangerous, most **EXTREME** or simply the most ridiculous challenge or stunt, MrBeast knows how to keep his fans coming back for more. And of course, offering lots of cash or exclusive merchandise as prizes helps too! The challenge and stunt sets are elaborate – with no expense spared – and the contestants are willing to push themselves to their limits. This is reality entertainment at its best – it's shocking and it's fun, and it's fascinating to see how people behave when they are put in extreme situations!

Let's look at some of the most popular MrBeast videos. . .

## EVERY COUNTRY ON EARTH FIGHTS FOR $250,000!

Beast Olympics was released on YouTube in August 2023. Contestants from all over the world competed to win $250,000 (£198,000). The events in the games included hurdles, an obstacle course, archery and football penalty kicks. In true MrBeast fashion, each game was set up with a twist – the gymnastic beams, for example, were set up more than 20 feet (6 metres) off the ground! Libya's contestant was the last person standing and walked away with the prize money.

> **"** I believe if you're smart enough, you can make money doing anything. **"**

# " Input inspiration, output ideas. "

## THE WORLD'S MOST DANGEROUS TRAP!

In this extreme challenge, contestant Mack had to try to beat a sequence of utterly outrageous obstacles. With each level he completed, he won $100,000 (£86,000). The obstacle course involved traps such as laser beams, giant boulders, high beams and a platforming style pathway in a giant hamster ball. Mack reached level 7, but lost $700,000 when he accidentally crumbled an umbrella-themed cookie in the Squid Game cookie challenge. Mack was so close that MrBeast let him keep $100,000 because he felt so bad for Mack's loss!

# THE WORLD'S DEADLIEST LASER MAZE!

In November 2023, MrBeast constructed the world's most perplexing laser maze. This labyrinth became more and more difficult with each level and featured moving laser walls, giant beams and obstacle courses. The contestant who survived the longest without triggering a laser, TikToker Breannah Yeh, won $250,000. This video reached more than 75 million views in its first week alone!

*"The rules are simple . . . you touch a laser, you lose $250,000!"*

> **"Work crazy hours when you feel like it, but then recharge."**

## ROCK, PAPER, SCISSORS!

In 2020, MrBeast created a rock, paper, scissors tournament stream that featured 32 YouTube influencers. The grand prize was $250,000 and was won by YouTube gamer Nadeshot.

A similar competition was run later, but this time the contestants were members of the public and the prize was $50,000. MrBeast must **REALLY LOVE** this game, because he then decided to run another rock, paper, scissors tournament on the back of the wrappers of his Feastables chocolate bars, open to the public. The best 16 players were invited to compete for the grand prize. The contestants then faced off in a best-of-three format.

Competition was tight, but the ultimate winner was Michael. MrBeast offered to double Michael's money by playing one last game (at the risk of losing it all), but Michael decided to walk away with the $50,000 (very wise!). And the losers didn't leave empty-handed either – they could select a package from a pile of boxes that each contained a secret prize.

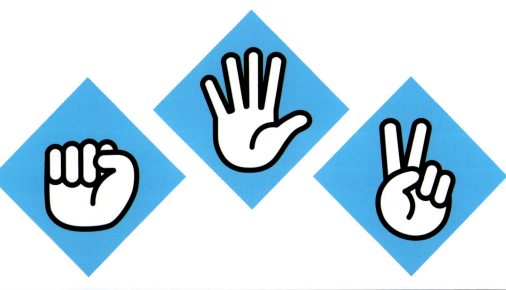

**Influencer Nadeshot threw rock to beat Casey Neistat's scissors in the final round in 2020.**

# I SPENT 7 DAYS BURIED ALIVE!

Not content with being **buried alive in a large coffin for 50 hours** in 2021, MrBeast decided he would shatter his own record by attempting to go **underground for a whole 7 days** in November 2023!

**WARNING! DO NOT TRY THIS AT HOME**

Every MrBeast stunt is carefully planned, assessed and monitored to keep all participants safe.

Surviving in the confined space meant that MrBeast had to pee into plastic bottles while suffering a bad back. It was physical and mental agony, and MrBeast broke down in tears several times. Just as for the 50-hour challenge, the Beast Gang kept in touch with Jimmy via walkie-talkies from above ground, and did their best to annoy their buddy while he was buried to see if they could force him to quit before the time was up.

"BRACE YOURSELF!"

But despite all of this, Jimmy kept his sense of humour and somehow survived the seven-day ordeal, emerging above ground a hero! He couldn't wait to be dug up, and shed tears of pure relief when the challenge was over. The first thing the gang said when they opened his coffin was how bad both it and Jimmy smelled! That first shower must have felt sooo good!

> **I always, always, always want to be improving my content ... The pacing, ideas, editing, scenes, jokes, execution, etc. can always be better ... I'll never get complacent.**

# 7 DAYS STRANDED AT SEA

Jimmy and four of his team – Kris, Nolan, Lazer and Tareq – challenged themselves to spend seven days stranded at sea on a raft. They all admitted that it was one of the hardest challenges any of them had completed. By the end of Day 1, they already wished they could go home!

Survival specialists had equipped the raft with all the materials the gang needed to build a shelter that would protect them from the sun and rain. They also had one small box of food supplies and two barrels of fresh drinking water that had to last them the whole seven days.

" The only time you should look back is to see how far you've come. "

The gang's first attempts to build the shelter didn't end very well – it wasn't weatherproof, and after several days of storms and a period of more than 20 hours of non-stop rain, they were soaking wet, cold, tired and feeling seasick. With tensions high, the whole crew wanted to quit the challenge. Then, with food and water supplies running low, and all attempts at fishing having failed, the gang eventually rallied together to rebuild the shelter.

The last couple of days on the raft were uncomfortably hot, but the gang's shelter was able to withstand the elements, and the friends struggled on, tired and hungry to the end.

All five members of the team said that the best thing about the challenge was leaving the raft, and hoped that they would never have to **poop in a bucket** ever again! Having to survive with very little made the team appreciate what they have in their everyday lives.

"BRYAN IS THE GOAT!"

Despite all the difficulties, there were several happy moments: a friendly seabird (nicknamed **Bryan**) visited the raft several times, an **ENORMOUS whale** swam near the vessel, and the gang will never forget the comforting taste of their first hot meal of canned chilli on Day 3!

# AGES 1–100 FIGHT FOR $500,000

In this challenge, **100 people aged between one and 100** were each put in their own glass cube, with 300 cameras recording their every move. The winner would be the person who stayed inside their cube the longest. During the experience, the contestants had to take part in different challenges which would result in some contestants having to leave. It proved to be an interesting study in human behaviour, as different age groups ganged together to try to oust other contestants.

Who's gonna win?

Within the first couple of hours, ten people left after the one – to ten-year-olds decided to make as much noise as they could in order to annoy everyone else. By **Day 2**, 76 people remained. After the first challenge of "guess which cup has the ball under it", a further 24 people were eliminated.

> **" The challenge has officially begun, let's see which age is the best! "**

With fewer contestants in the game, tensions were beginning to rise, and people started targeting individual players to try to vote them out: ages 54 and 74 proved to be very unpopular!

On **Day 4**, ten players were voted out by the other contestants, leaving 25 people in the challenge. The players in their 50s worked together to get rid of some of the contestants in their 70s.

By the end of **Day 5**, after a Jenga challenge, only ten people remained (the youngest was aged 19 and the oldest was 54) – everyone over the age of 60 had been eliminated!

On **Day 7**, the final ten contestants had to play a game of marbles. The five winners were aged 23, 40, 43, 52 and 54. The 95 contestants already out of the game voted on the three players they wanted to eliminate. Ages 23, 43 and 54 had to leave.

On **Day 8**, the final day, the two remaining contestants, aged 40 and 52, had to play a game of bluff to win the **$500,000 prize**. Each player had a suitcase in front of them, one of which contained the prize money. Player 40 had to look in his suitcase and then "bluff" whether or not the money was inside. Player 52 had to try to work out the truth by asking him a series of questions. Was Player 40 bluffing? Was the money in his case or her own? After careful deliberation, Player 52 guessed it was in her closed suitcase, but she was wrong! Player 40 had successfully bluffed his way to a **cool $500,000 payday**!

# $1 VERSUS MILLIONS OF DOLLARS!

Other popular videos on the MrBeast channels are ones where he compares cheap products with those costing mega bucks. Some of the results are surprising, and not what you would expect – the most expensive items are not always the best!

He once fed a lucky cat $10 vs $10,000 sushi. Which one do you think the cat preferred?

$1 vs $1,000,000,000  Yacht House Car

$1 vs $10,000,000  Job

$1 vs $1,000,000  Hotel room

$1 vs $500,000  Plane ticket

$1 vs $250,000  Vacation

*"No matter how big the videos get, I want to go bigger."*

> **" The only competition you have is the person you were yesterday. "**

## MILLION-DOLLAR STUNTS

MrBeast loves to shock his viewers by thinking up the most bizarre stunts. Any Lamborghini lovers out there were probably horrified to see the video where MrBeast dropped this classic (not to mention, expensive) supercar into the world's largest shredder. It took a few attempts, but the car got shredded in the end!

In another stunt video, MrBeast runs a train off its tracks into a giant pit! And how about the time he challenged a contestant to build a barrier to protect a car, while he fired rockets at it from a tank? The car actually survived the assault!

Such stunts take plenty of planning, money and time to set up, but the end results are always very watchable (well, unless it was your train or car!).

Critics say that stunts like these are an extravagant waste of money. While this may be true, the videos attract a lot of sponsorship, and MrBeast donates a large part of the money raised to his charitable projects. Is it any different from a car being shredded to make a blockbuster movie?

# THE BEAST GANG

Jimmy as MrBeast is a unique phenomenon, but he couldn't have reached his **megastar YouTuber status** without a lot of help from his friends, family and colleagues.

As of 2023, the MrBeast team is made up of more than **250 people**, including Jimmy himself. Everyone has a role to play in the brainstorming, planning, set-ups, staging, filming and production of all the MrBeast videos, charity projects and events. As you can imagine, a massive amount of work, time, effort and money goes into every video that appears on the MrBeast channels.

But it is Jimmy's group of closest friends who help him run the MrBeast empire and co-host his videos with him. Introducing the **Beast Gang!**

*Some of the Beast Gang hang out at the launch of MrBeast Burger in 2022.*

> **" I'm motivated because I want to employ my friends and help them. "**

### KRIS TYSON
**Date of Birth:** 1 July, 1996
Kris and Jimmy have been **best friends** since their schooldays. They would sit together at lunch, chatting about YouTube and video games. They would hang out together out of school and film videos, too. They have been friends for more than 15 years. Kris was there when Jimmy created his channel, and she was his first subscriber. Kris co-hosts the MrBeast channels with Jimmy and is the main host of **Beast Reacts**. Kris has her own followers on Instagram and X (formerly Twitter) and a channel on Twitch. She has a son and is currently the only member of the gang who is a parent.

## CHANDLER HALLOW

**Date of Birth:** 3 December, 1998
Chandler worked as a janitor for MrBeast, before becoming a social media celebrity in his own right. He was offered a small role in one of MrBeast's videos. The viewers loved him, and he soon became a Beast Gang favourite, appearing regularly in new videos. As well as featuring on MrBeast's TikTok channel, Chandler has his own Instagram and TikTok accounts, with millions of followers.

## KARL JACOBS

**Date of Birth:** 19 July, 1998
Karl started out as an editor for Jimmy's brother C.J., and then became a camera operator for Jimmy, before appearing in MrBeast videos. As well as all his work on MrBeast, Karl has his own YouTube channels – **@Karl** and **Pixel Playground**, where he plays, comments on and makes challenges for online games like **Roblox** and **Minecraft**.

> **Surround yourself with people you want to be.**

### NOLAN HANSEN
**Date of Birth:** 1 June, 1998
Nolan was the last member to join the inner MrBeast circle. Before he met Jimmy, he had his own YouTube channel **TrendCrave**, where he posted commentaries on a variety of Top-5 and Top-10 YouTube videos. He is now a regular in MrBeast videos and often co-hosts or takes part in challenges.

# BEAST REACTS

**SUBSCRIBE FOR A COOKIE!**

Together, Kris and Jimmy make up the epic duo that hosts **Beast Reacts**. They film their reactions to some of the internet's favourite videos to hilarious comic effect. And they get to learn some interesting facts along the way. Like these gems, for example:

### DID YOU KNOW?

About one in 750 people have an extra finger on each hand – that's 7.5 million people altogether in the world, so an extra 15 million fingers out there, just wiggling around! #rarestthingsonearth

### DID YOU KNOW?

There is a 1 in 1,120 chance of seeing a 360-degree rainbow and a 1 in 5,000 chance of a tiger having a black coat with orange stripes, rather than the reverse. Wow!

> "If you're watching this, life is good. Just remember that."

# BEAST GAMING

**SUBSCRIBE ... OR ELSE!**

Jimmy is a fanatical gamer. He uses his **Beast Gaming** channel to turn his favourite online games into epic challenges like "If You Build It, I'll Pay For It" or "Press This Button" – with a huge cash prize often involved! Jimmy and the Beast Gang comment on the progress of players or try to help them. They all love playing *Minecraft* and *Call of Duty: Black Ops II* in co-op.

**ONLY REAL GAMERS CAN SUBSCRIBE!**

"I've got 100 Minecraft players and whatever they build, I'll pay for."

# BEAST
# PHILANTHROPY

Jimmy created his **Beast Philanthropy** YouTube channel in 2020. He says, "My overarching goal in life is to make a lot of money and then before I die, give it away." His acts of kindness and generosity resonate with his audience. Whether he is giving away free clothes, providing meals to the homeless, setting up a food bank, paying for eye surgeries or establishing a free children's hospital, Jimmy's genuine empathy and compassion shine through.

Jimmy has received a lot of hate from people asking how his acts of generosity can be truly selfless when he makes so much money from the videos and publicity they generate. However, Jimmy believes that by publicizing his charitable projects through his videos, not only does he help those in need, but he also generates public awareness and positive publicity, which means others are more likely to donate, sponsor or take part in fundraisers themselves. And 100% of any money he makes from the channel funds more charity work.

> **Help others and give back.
> It's the only way to be truly successful.**

Just some of MrBeast's philanthropic projects:

- Gave away 10,000 turkeys in his hometown, Greenville
- Donated 20,000 pairs of shoes to children in Africa
- Gifted $300,000 worth of tech to various schools
- Delivered $100,000 worth of supplies to homeless shelters
- Built wells in Africa that supply fresh drinking water
- Saved an orphanage in South Africa from closure
- Rebuilt houses for tornado survivors in Kentucky, USA

> **I want to make money so later on
> in life I can do big things.**

# #TEAMTREES

Did you know that nearly **half of the world's trees have been destroyed** since the start of human civilization? Trees are vital to the environment and so many aspects of our lives. They provide oxygen for us to breathe and clean the air by soaking up harmful carbon dioxide from the planet, helping to combat climate change. Trees play an important role in the water cycle, which helps to provide us with clean water. Homes for humans and habitats for wildlife as well as fuel can be created from trees, and these natural wonders protect land against flooding and erosion.

In 2019, MrBeast and former NASA engineer and YouTuber **Mark Rober**, announced that they were going to launch a fundraising challenge event on YouTube called **#TeamTrees**. Their goal was to raise $20 million (about £16.5 million) for the Arbor Day Foundation by 1 January, 2020, and to plant trees no later than December 2022. One tree would be planted for every dollar donated.

The response online was phenomenal, with other celebrity YouTubers shining a light on the project. Trees began to be planted in US national parks. The original goal of 20 million trees was quickly met, and as of October 2023, more than **24 million trees** had been planted all around the world. Incredible!

## PLANTING RESPONSIBLY

It is important to plant the right species of tree in the correct habitat, as planting trees in the wrong places can actually damage ecosystems, increase wildfire intensity and add to global warming. If you want to take part in tree replanting, contact the organizations that do this (a quick internet search will list them), and find out where you can help in your local area.

# #TEAMSEAS

The huge clean-up project **#TeamSeas** is another important environmental project that MrBeast has embraced. In 2021, Jimmy and Mark Rober organized a second collaborative challenge. This time, the goal was to raise **$30 million** (almost £25 million) for the Ocean Conservancy and the Ocean Cleanup organizations. They pledged to fund the **removal of 13,600 tonnes of plastic** and other waste from oceans, rivers and beaches by 1 January, 2022.

Once again, the response was staggering, and **#TeamSeas** met its target. As of October 2023, more than **15,000 tonnes of rubbish** globally had been removed from seas, oceans and other bodies of water.

Oceans around the world are littered with discarded fishing gear, plastic and other waste, with rivers a major source of this pollution. Research shows that just 1% of rivers account for nearly 80% of the pollution that flows from them into our planet's seas and oceans. **#TeamSeas** continues to remove this rubbish and dispose of it responsibly.

### THE IMPORTANCE OF OUR OCEANS

Oceans and seas cover more than **70% of Earth's surface**. These incredible bodies of water help to regulate our climate and generate most of the oxygen we breathe (from oceanic plankton). They also provide us with food. But as a result of human activity, our oceans are being harmed. Every year, an estimated eight million tonnes of plastic waste ends up in the sea. Overfishing threatens fish stocks, while sewage pollution and climate change are damaging the key marine ecosystems, killing marine life and coral reefs.

If you live near the sea or a river (or even if you don't), contact local environmental organizations to find out how you can get involved in beach, ocean or river clean-ups.

# BEAST BUSINESS

Not only is Jimmy a **YouTube superstar**, but he is also a successful entrepreneur and businessman. He is the founder of **MrBeast Burger** (a fast-food brand) and **Feastables** (a confectionery brand), and the co-creator of **#TeamTrees** and **#TeamSeas**. He also sells exclusive MrBeast merch online.

Jimmy is always looking to invest his money in other projects about which he is passionate. In 2022, MrBeast and East Carolina University announced a partnership to train students to work in creative industries and become online content creators.

A young fan grabs a selfie with their hero, MrBeast, at a rare public appearance.

# MRBEAST BURGER

MrBeast joined forces with Virtual Dining Concepts to create the super cool (and delicious!) **MrBeast Burger** – a virtual restaurant brand. Participating restaurants across the United States can prepare and sell MrBeast Burgers from their existing kitchens. Customers can order from the MrBeast Burger menu on the app (or through other major food-delivery apps) and get their burger delivered directly to their door!

Check out some of the **tasty burgers** on offer on the menu – **Beast Style**, **Chandler Style**, **Chris Style** and **Karl's Deluxe**! Which meaty treat would you order?

## BEAST STYLE

Smashed crispy beef patties with house seasoning, American cheese, diced pickles, white onion, mayo, ketchup and brown mustard on a toasted bun.

## CHANDLER STYLE

Two smashed crispy beef patties with house seasoning, served plain with American cheese on a toasted bun.

## CHRIS STYLE

Two smashed crispy beef patties with house seasoning, American cheese, bacon, topped with crinkle fries on a toasted bun.

## KARL'S DELUXE

A patty melt served Karl's Style with crispy seasoned beef patty, caramelized onions and American cheese on a toasted flipped bun.

*"Dream as big as you want to, and never apologize for it."*

# FEASTABLES

Who doesn't like chocolate? Certainly not MrBeast! In 2022, Jimmy started a new food company called **Feastables**. He launched with his own-brand chocolate bars called MrBeast Bars, in three flavours – Original, Almond and Quinoa Crunch. The chocolate bars became so popular that MrBeast expanded the range! As well as the original flavours, Deez Nutz, Crunch and Milk Chocolate bars later went on sale around the world.

**Karl Gummies** in sour green apple and sour blue raspberry flavours, and **MrBeast Cookies** in two varieties – peanut butter chocolate chip and chocolate chip – were the next additions to the Feastables range.

## DID YOU KNOW?

MrBeast's Feastables chocolate bars are both plant-based and gluten free. Within the first 72 hours of its launch, the brand sold more than **one million chocolate bars**!

Jimmy combined the launch of Feastables with various online sweepstakes and video challenges and over $1 million in prizes. Ten lucky winners even got to compete to win a chocolate factory! The video "I built Willy Wonka's Chocolate Factory" featured the famous British chef Gordon Ramsay as a cake judge and offered a $500,000 (about £411,500) cash prize.

"I want to build Feastables, Beast Burger, etc. and eventually be able to sell parts of them for billions of dollars, so I can give away billions in future videos."

# AND THE WINNER IS...?

MrBeast wouldn't be where he is today without his **millions of dedicated fans**. The following awards show just how much they love what he does, as well as the impact and influence his channels have. His list of honours grows every year – we just hope he has a trophy cabinet big enough for all these awards!

„ If it gets the most views, it's because people click on it, and I want to give them what they want. "

> **"Work hard and do what you love... eventually the right person will notice you."**

### The Streamy Awards: WINNER!

**2023**
Creator of the Year
Best Collaboration (with Dwayne 'The Rock' Johnson)

**2022**
Creator of the Year
Social Good: Creator
Brand Engagement

**2021**
Creator of the Year

**2020**
Creator of the Year
Social Good: Nonprofit or NGO
Social Good: Creator
Live Special

**2019**
Breakout Creator

### Nickelodeon Kids' Choice Awards, USA: WINNER!

**2023** Favourite Male Creator

**2022** Favourite Male Creator

### YouTube Creator Awards: WINNER!

**2021** Creator of the Year

### Shorty Awards: WINNER!

**2020** YouTuber of the Year

### Guinness World Records

**2023** First person to reach 1 million followers on Threads

**2022** Largest vegetarian burger

**2022** Most subscribers for an individual male on YouTube

**2021** Highest-earning YouTube contributor

# THE MAN BEHIND THE BEAST

MrBeast may appear as the life and soul of the party in his videos, but out of the spotlight Jimmy is a very private person. He describes himself as an **introvert**, and he likes to keep his offline life just that – **offline**.

Little is known about him when he is not being MrBeast. His obsession with YouTube, his intense work ethic and the incredibly long hours he works make days off pretty tricky. It is public knowledge that as of October 2023 he was dating the gaming streamer **Thea Booysen**. It is also known that he suffers from **Crohn's disease**, a lifelong condition where parts of the digestive system become inflamed. Other than that, Jimmy has successfully managed to keep his private life under wraps.

MrBeast and Thea pose together at the Nickelodeon Kids' Choice Awards in 2023.

In an interview with podcasters Colin and Samir, MrBeast said that he sometimes **struggles with work-life balance**. When he is tired, he takes a couple of hours off to watch anime. He is a **huge anime fan** and LOVES *Naruto*. In the Japanese dubbed version of MrBeast's viral *Squid Game* video, fans recognized a familiar voice. They were amazed to find out that MrBeast was voiced by Naruto's Japanese voice actor, Junko Takeuchi!

" Don't take yourself too seriously. Life is too short to stress over things you can't control. "

> **" Don't let other people tell you what to do with your life. "**

As MrBeast, Jimmy tries to stay neutral when it comes to politics. He much prefers talking about his charity work and his personal goals to help as many people as he can in his lifetime. One of his goals is to feed hundreds of millions of people through his projects, which is why he has set up a licensed charity that functions as a food bank, feeding communities across the United States.

In a podcast in 2022, Jimmy stated that he would consider **running for president** in the future, as he believes the US would benefit from a more youthful presidency.

It is hard to be famous without attracting some controversy and negativity, though. MrBeast's videos have attracted a wide range of reactions; some applaud his generosity and philanthropy, while others believe he exploits his platform for his own gain and recognition.

MrBeast still loves YouTube, and his passion for making videos has not faded. On the podcast The Colin and Samir Show, he said, **"I'm 25, and I love it more than when I was 19!"**

His camera collection has now grown to between 250 and 300, with many of his videos requiring multiple shots from multiple angles. Some videos have needed more than 50 cameras alone, which is why his huge collection is necessary!

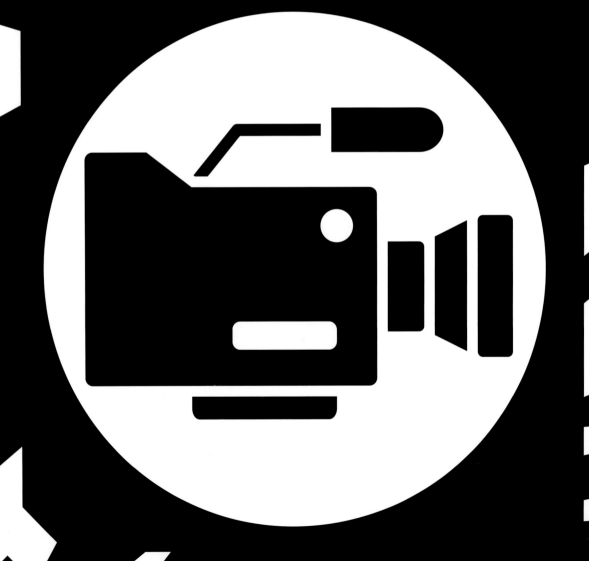

MrBeast has transformed the way that video content is created. Who'd have guessed that by simply counting to 100,000 just a few years ago, Jimmy would be catapulted towards global super stardom?

His journey is simply phenomenal: he has shattered records, helped combat climate change, donated millions of dollars to worthy causes, created new brands and businesses . . . the list goes on. So what does the future hold? Well, we know for certain that the videos are going to be just as big, if not even **WACKIER** than ever. The giveaways are going to be equally **EPIC** and there will no doubt be other records to break. Stay tuned.

**"** I appreciate all of you. **"**

# PICTURE CREDITS

While every effort has been made to credit all contributors, we would like to apologize should there be any omissions or errors, and would be pleased to make any appropriate corrections for future editions of this book.

## Cover:

Denise Truscello/Getty Images

## Interiors:

**Creative Commons:** 34, 58 Fidias; 44, 63 Nick Rewind

**Getty Images:** 5, 6, 14 Ethan Pines/The Forbes Collection Contour RA; 8–9, 23 Steve Granitz /FilmMagic; 10–11 Sopa Images; 13, 43, 64 Denise Truscello; 19 Vivien Killilea/Getty Images for TikTok; 20, 63 Kevin Mazur; 24 Frazer Harrison; 28 Jeff Kravitz; 38, 40, 41, 50, 51, 52 Dave Kotinsky; 39 Gregg DeGuire /Getty Images for Nickelodeon; 46, 48 Noam Galai/Getty Images for YouTube; 55 Ethan Miller; 56 Roy Rochlin/Getty Images for YouTube; 59 Mark Von Holden/ Variety via Getty Images; 60 SOPA Images.

**Shutterstock.com:** 16 Mehaniq; 37 Mirage_studio; 54 The Image Party.